Learn Spanish for Beginners & Dummies

By Glenn Nora

By going through this document, the reader understands and agrees that in any situation is the author is not responsible for any kind of direct or indirect losses that might occur because of the use of the information contained in this document, including, but not limited to, —inaccuracies, errors, or omissions.

Table of Contents

Conclusion

Introduction

Hola, the following chapters will get you started on your endeavor to learn the Spanish language. First you will become familiar with the alphabet, then you will learn the common verbs and how to use them in a sentence.

The natural progression of learning will occur as you move through this book; this means that as you learn to modify verbs, use adjectives, and become familiar with common accents and intonations, you will find yourself forming proper Spanish sentences in no time. This book will provide you with an easy read to get you started on the path to learning, speaking, reading, and writing Spanish.

This is an excellent resource specifically for beginners looking to learn Spanish. With the concepts and vocabulary available to you, you will be able to speak and read the Spanish language at a basic level.

Take every opportunity to practice your new skills; listen and recognize words and phrases spoken by others and attempt to join in on their conversations. Ask them for feedback on your speaking. This book seeks to provide you with an enjoyable experience as learning a new language like Spanish can be easy and fun.

Chapter 1: Letters of the Alphabet and Pronunciation

The most basic part of the Spanish language is the alphabet. By learning how letters sound, you will be able to begin the process of learning to speak Spanish. Each letter has a different sound. As you read through the alphabet, you will find that most letters have the same sound in both Spanish and English.

A few of the letters in Spanish are not found in the English language alphabet. With practice, you will be able to understand the letters when you hear them.

On the next page there is a chart of all the letters of the Spanish alphabet with their pronunciation. After going through all the letters, you will begin to have an "ear" for the language and be on your way to speaking and understanding Spanish.

Spanish Alphabet

Letter	Name of Letter	Pronunciation
a	A	Pronounced like "a" in latte
b	Be	Pronounced like "b" in bull
c	Ce	When followed by an "i" or "e" the sounds like the "c" in cellophane, by other vowels like the "c" in camp.
ch	Che	Pronounced like the "ch" in each
d	De	Pronounced like "d" in dingo
e	E	Pronounced like "e" in fey
f	Efe	Pronounced like "f" in father
g	Ge	If followed by an "i" or "e" pronounced like the "h" in hen, otherwise, Pronounced like "g"

		in gum
h	hache	The letter "h" not pronounced when at the beginning of a word.
i	I	Pronounced like "ee" like in meet
j	Jota	Pronounced like "h" in hit.
k	Ka	Not a Spanish language letter. Used in foreign works like "karate"
l	Ele	Pronounced like the "l" in lettuce
ll	Elle	Pronounced like "y" in yams
m	Eme	Pronounced as one pronounces the "m" as mountain
n	Ene	Pronounced as one pronounces the "n" as news
ñ	Eñe	Pronounced like "ny" in

		banyan
o	O	Pronounced like "o" in north
p	Pe	Pronounced as one pronounces "p" as pop
q	Cu	Just like English, followed by a "u" - 'qu' is followed by an "i" or an "e." It is pronounced like the letter "k" as key
r	Ere	Pronounced like "r" in run
rr	Erre	Pronounced like "rr" in barrier. This letter utilizes the roll of the tongue when pronouncing the sound of "rr"
s	Ese	Pronounced like "s" in second
t	Te	Pronounced like "t" in toast
u	U	Pronounced like "u" in unique
v	Ve	Pronounced like "b" best

w	doble ve	Not a Spanish language letter. Used in foreign works like "whisky"
x	equis	Pronounced like "x" in examine
y	igriega	Pronounced like "y" in yen
z	Zeta	Pronounced like "th" in think

Only a few of the letters have more than one sound. Memorize the pronunciation of the letters, and you will be able to understand when Spanish is spoken to you. Practice the sounds so that the words you see and hear are natural to speak and understand. Become a master at pronunciation, and you will feel the natural ease of speaking the new language.

Don't be afraid to practice your pronunciation with native Spanish speakers, if possible. This will be the best practice of all. You will be able to mimic the exact sounds made by native speakers and become comfortable with hearing the language being spoken as well. Practicing listening and speaking Spanish will make you more successful, faster.

When Vowels are Grouped Together

For words that have vowels grouped together, the individual letters are pronounced in the same what that they are when they stand alone. Use the same pronunciation for each letter. Just merge them together quickly so that the sounds of the three letters are blended. A word like huevos (eggs), will sound like oo-eh-vo or **whay-v**o.

When you practice pronunciation, keep in mind that you will be blending the sounds into one continuous sound with each individual letter pronounced. This is true for words like viaje (trip), which will sound like vee-**a**-hah. Speak the letters individually but blend them into one sound. It will become natural.

Accents and Intonations

When reading words, take note of the structure of the word so that you will know how to pronounce the word. The basic rule is that if that words ending in the letter "n," "s," or a vowel, the second to last syllable is stressed. For words where this is not the case, pronounce the inflection on the last syllable.

This is common for the infinitive form of verbs, as well as other words. If there is an accent mark in the word, that indicates the syllable to be stressed.

This includes words like:

aquí (here)
árbol(tree)
canción (song)
cárcel (jail)
débil (weak)
exámenes (exams)
inglés (English)
también (also)

Some words have a spelling with an accent and a spelling without an accent. There is a different meaning to the word spelled with an accent than the word spelled without an accent.

como (I eat/like or as) (how?)	¿cómo?
el (the)	él (he)
se (indirect object pronoun)	sé (I know)
si (if)	sí (yes)
te (object: you)	té: (tea)
tu (your)	tú (you)
como (I eat/like or as) (how?)	¿cómo?

Some words, when used as questions, always use an accent mark:

The word ¿cómo? translates as how? or why?
The word ¿cuál? translates as which?
The word ¿cuándo? translates as when?
The word ¿cuánto? translates as how much? or how many?
The word ¿dónde? translates as where?

The word ¿por qué? translates as why?
The word ¿qué? translates as what?
The word ¿quién? translates as who?

Without a question mark, the word is no longer a question and becomes a pronoun or an object. See the alternate uses of the words and the spelling below:

Spanish	English
¿Cómo estás?	How are you?
¿Cuál canción es tu favorita	Which song is your favorite?
¿Cuándo comes el pastel?	When will you eat the cake?
¿Cuánto cuesta?	How much is it?
¿Dónde está la playa?	Where Is the beach?
¿Por qué?	Why?
¿Cuál son tus zapatos?	Which are your shoes?
¿Quién es ese?	Who is that?

Spanish	English
Yo se como estas.	I know how you are.
Escuché esa canción, que me hace feliz.	I heard that song, which makes me happy.
Iré a la fiesta cuando termine de comer.	I will go to the party when I finish eating.
Ya veo cuanto comprar.	I see how much to buy.
Estoy en la playa donde la arena es blanca.	I am at the beach where the sand is white.
Porque.	Because.
Yo se cual.	I know which one.
Ella sabe quien es.	She knows who that is.

When the question word is asking a question, there is an accent. When the question word is used as a noun, pronoun or object, the accent is not used.

Chapter 2: Verbs

Infinitive Tense

This is the basic form of a verb. It starts the word "to;" to run, to eat, to talk, etc. The Spanish verbs have specific endings in the infinitive tense. Some verbs have the last two letters of ""ar," many have the last two letter that are "er," and others have the last two lettrs of "ir." These action words are conjugated, or assigned a gender and number, according to the verb ending. The infinitive tense may also be used in its unconjugated form when it is not used as a verb in the sentence.

- The infinitive tense can be a noun or the subject of a sentence:

Spanish	English
Mentir es malo.	Lying is bad.
Comer te hace feliz.	Eating makes you happy.
Correr es saludable.	Running is healthy.
Estudiar es necesario.	Studying is necessary.

You can see that the infinitive form of the verb becomes the noun.

- The infinitive form of the verb can also be used in a sentence following the conjugated form:

Spanish	English
Tienen que escribir	They have to write
Ella espera verlo	She is waiting to see him
Gladis le encanta bailar.	Gladis loves to dance.
Nosotros vamos caer.	We are going to fall.

- The infinitive form may be preceded by a preposition or may simply be the infinitive form of a verb.

- The infinitive form of the verb is also used when it is a clause following the main clause when the subject is the same or implied:

Spanish	English
Tiene miedo de esquiar.	He is afraid of skiing.
Se levantó temprano para desayunar.	She woke up early to eat breakfast.
No queremos comer.	We don't want to eat.
Es malo robar.	It's bad to steal.

Conjugations of Verbs

In Spanish, verbs are usually changed to have an appropriate ending that corresponds to the correct subject and of the clause in which the verb is being used. This process is called conjugation. The verb ending is changed to give information about who is performing the action in addition to when the action is performed. The reference to "when" is related to the tense of the verb.

How the verb is conjugated depends on whether the verb ends in -ar, -er, or -ir.

Present Tense of Verbs

The present tense of verbs describes something taking place in the current moment. It is the most common tense used.

Present Tense	English	Spanish	"ar"	"er"	"ir"
1st Singular	I	yo	- o	- o	- o
2nd Singular	You (familiar)	tú	- as	- es	- es
3rd Singular	You (formal), he, she, it	usted, él, ella, el	- a	- e	- e
1st Plural	We	nosotros, nosotras	- amos	- emos	- imos
2nd Plural	You all (familiar)	vosotros, vosotras	- áis	- éis	- ís
3rd Plural	You (formal), they	ustedes, ellos, ellas	- an	- en	- en

The regular conjugation is presented below:

Tense	English	-ar llegar	-er comer	-ir vivir
1st Singular	I	llego (I speak)	como (I eat)	vivo (I live)
2nd Singular	You (familiar)	llegas (you speak)	comes (you eat)	vives (you live)
3rd Singular	You (formal), he, she, it	llega (You, he, she arrive/s)	come (You, he, she eat/s)	vive (You live)
1st Plural	We	llegamos (we arrive)	comemos (we eat)	vivimos (we live)
2nd Plural	You all (familiar)	llegáis (you all arrive)	coméis (you all eat)	vivís (you all live)
3rd Plural	You (formal), they	llegan (You, they arrive)	comen (You, they eat)	viven (You, they live)

Regular verbs are verbs that use the standard conjugation to modify the form of the verb.

-ar	-er	-ir
acabar (finish)	aprender (learn)	compartir (share)
aceptar (accept)	comer (eat)	cumplir (fulfill, carry out)
ayudar (help)	comprender (comprehend)	decidir (decide)

cambiar (change)
considerar (consider)
crear (create)
crucificar (crucify)
dejar (leave, allow)
entrar (enter, come in)
escuchar (listen, hear)

esplinar

estudiar (study)
gastar (spend)
gustar (like)
hablar (speak)
levantar (raise, lift)
llamar (call, name)
llevar (bring, carry)
mirar (look, watch)
necesitar (need)
pasar (spend time, pass)
preguntar (ask, inquire)
presentar (introduce)
quedar (remain, stay)
resultar (result)
terminar (end)
tomar (drink,

correr (run)

deber (owe, must)

meter (put, place)

pretender (attempt)
responder (respond, answer)
suceder (happen, succeed)

vender (sell)

discutir (discuss, argue)

existir (exist)

insistir (insist)
ocurrir (happen, occur)
partir (divide, leave)
permitir (permit, allow)
recibir (receive, greet)
subir (rise up)
vivir (live)

take)			
trabajar (work)			
tratar (try)			
usar (use)			

There are several verbs that do not follow the regular conjugation. They have various conjugations that may or may not be similar to other words. Many of these verbs with irregular conjugation are words used commonly within the Spanish language.

- Verbs that end in -guir, change the 1st person singular ending -go. for example, the 1st person singular of the word extinguir is "yo extingo."

- You will see verbs with endings of -ger and also the verb ending of -gir. These have a slightly different treatment. The 1st person singular ending is -jo. for example, the 1st person singular present tense for dirigir is "yo dirijo."

Present Tense	English	Spanish	Ser (be)	Estar (be)	Ir (go)
1st Singular	I	yo	soy	estoy	voy
2nd Sing	You (fam	tú	eres	estás	vas

ular	iliar)				
3rd Singular	You (formal), he, she, it	usted, él, ella, el	es	está	va
1st Plural	We	nosotros, nosotras	somos	estamos	vamos
2nd Plural	You all (familiar)	vosotros, vosotras	sois	estáis	váis
3rd Plural	You (formal), they	ustedes, ellos, ellas	son	Están	van

Present Tense	English	Spanish	Haber (have to)	Hacer (make, do)	Decir (say)
1st Singular	I	yo	he	hago	digo
2nd Singular	You (familiar)	tú	has	haces	dices
3rd Singular	You (formal), he, she, it	usted, él, ella, el	ha, hay	hace	dice

1st Plural	We	nosotros, nosotras	he mos	hace mos	deci mos
2nd Plural	You all (familiar)	vosotros, vosotras	hab éis	hacé is	decí s
3rd Plural	You (formal), they	ustedes, ellos, ellas	han	hace n	dice n

Present Tense	English	Spanish	Tener (have)	Poner (put)	Sentir (feel)	Seguir (continue)
1st Singular	I	yo	ten go	pon go	sien to	sigo
2nd Singular	You (familiar)	tú	tien es	pon es	sien tes	sigues
3rd Singular	You (formal), he, she, it	usted, él, ella, el	tien e	pon e	sien te	sigue
1st Plural	We	nosotros, nosotras	tene mos	pon emo s	sent imo s	segui mos
2nd Plural	You all (familiar)	vosotros, vosotras	tené is	pon éis	sent ís	seguís

3rd Plural	You (formal), they	ustedes, ellos, ellas	tienen	ponen		
					sienten	siguen

Here is a list of words that are irregular in their conjugation:

-ar	-er	-ir
estar (be;temporary)	aparecer (appear)	abrir (open)
buscar (look for)		conducir (drive, conduct)
comenzar (commence)	caer (fall)	conseguir (get, obtain)
contar (count, tell a story)	conocer (know; people, places)	construir (construct)
	crecer (grow)	convertir (convert)
dar (give)	creer (believe)	
empezar (begin)	desaparecer (disappear)	cubrir (cover)
encontrar (find)	detener (stop, arrest)	decir (say, tell)
explicar (explain)	entender (understand)	descubrir (discover)
jugar (play a game or sport)	haber (have to do something)	dirigir (direct)
llegar (arrive)	hacer (do, make)	dormir (sleep)
pagar (pay)	leer (read)	elegir (choose)
pensar (think)	mover (move)	escribir (write)
recordar (remember)		impedir (prevent)
	nacer (be born)	
	obtener obtain, get	
	poner (place)	incluir (include)
sacar (take out)	paracer (appear)	intervenir (intervene)
tocar (play an instument)	ofrecer (offer)	
	parecer (seem,	ir (go)

	appear)	
		morir (die)
	poder (can)	oír (hear)
	perder (lose)	pedir (ask for)
	proponer (propose)	preferir (prefer)
	querer (love, want)	producir (produce)
		referir (refer (to))
	recoger (pick up)	
	reconocer (recognize)	repetir (repeat)
		salir (leave, go out)
	resolver (solve)	
		seguir (follow, continue)
	romper (break)	sentir (feel, regret)
	saber (know; something)	
	ser (be; permanent state)	servir (serve)
	soler (be accustomed to)	sufrir (suffer)
	suponer (suppose)	venir (come)
	tener (have)	
	traer (bring, carry)	
	valer (be worth)	
	ver (see)	
	volver (return)	

Past Tense of Verbs

Past Tense	English	Spanish	-ar	-er	-ir
1st Per Sing	I	yo	-é	-í	-í
2nd Per Sing	You (familiar)	tú	-aste	-iste	-iste
3rd Per Sing	You (formal), he, she, it	usted, él, ella, el	-ó	-ió	-ió
1st Plural	We	nosotros, nosotras	-amos	-imos	-imos
2nd Plural	You all (familiar)	vosotros, vosotras	-asteis	-isteis	-isteis
3rd Plural	You (formal), they	ustedes, ellos, ellas	-aron	-ieron	-ieron

The regular conjugation is presented below:

Tense	English	-ar hablar (speak)	-er comer (eat)	-ir vivir (live)
1st Singular	I	hablé (I spoke)	comí (I ate)	viví (I lived)
2nd Singular	You (familiar)	hablas (you spoke)	Comiste (you ate)	viviste (you live)
3rd Sin	You (form	habló (You,	comió (You,	vivió (You lived)

26

gul ar	al), he, she, it	**he, she spoke)**	**he, she ate)**	
1st Plural	We	**hablamos (we spoke)**	**comimos (we ate)**	**vivimos (we lived)**
2nd Plural	You all (familiar)	**hablasteis (you all spoke)**	**comisteis (you all ate)**	**vivisteis (you all lived)**
3rd Plural	You (formal), they	**hablaron (You, they spoke)**	**comieron (You, they ate)**	**vivieron (You, they lived)**

Past Tense	English	Spanish	Ser (be)	Estar (be)	Ir (go)
1st Singular	I	yo	fui	estuve	fui
2nd Singular	You (familiar)	tú	fuiste	estuviste	fuiste
3rd Singular	You (formal), he, she, it	usted, él, ella, el	fue	estuvo	fue
1st Plural	We	nosotros, nosotras	fuimos	estuvimos	fuimos
2nd Plural	You all (familiar)	vosotros, vos	fuisteis	estuvisteis	fuisteis

27

		otras			
3rd Plural	You (formal), they	ustedes, ellos, ellas	fueron	estuvieron	fueron

Past Tense	English	Spanish	Haber (have to)	Hacer (make, do)	Decir (say)
1st Singular	I	yo	hube	hice	dije
2nd Singular	You (familiar)	tú	hubiste	hiciste	dijiste
3rd Singular	You (formal), he, she, it	usted, él, ella, el	hubo	hizo	dijo
1st Plural	We	nosotros, nosotras	hubimos	hicimos	dijimos
2nd Plural	You all (familiar)	vosotros, vosotras	hubisteis	hicisteis	dijisteis
3rd Plural	You (form	ustedes,	hubieron	hicieron	dijeron

		ello s, ella s				
al), they						

Past Tense	English	Spanish	Tener (have)	Poner (put)	Sentir (feel)	Seguir (continue)
1st Singular	I	yo	tuve	puse	sentí	seguí
2nd Singular	You (familiar)	tú	tuviste	pusiste	sentiste	seguiste
3rd Singular	You (formal), he, she, it	usted, él, ella, el	tuvo	puso	sintió	siguió
1st Plural	We	nosotros, nosotras	tuvimos	pusimos	sentimos	seguimos
2nd Plural	You all (familiar)	vosotros, vosotras	tuvisteis	pusisteis	sentisteis	seguisteis
3rd Plural	You (formal), they	ustedes, ellos, ellas	tuvieron	pusieron	sintieron	siguieron

Chapter 3: What is the Subject? A Noun.

It's time to look at the most important part of speech--the noun. A noun and a verb are necessary to form a sentence. The noun is the subject of the sentence. It can be a person or location. It can also be an animal or an object; the sentence has to be about something, and that something is a noun. It is usually placed before the verb in a sentence.

Because it is such a common placement, the subject of a sentence is easily identifiable. When the noun is referred to in a generic way, like he, she or it, the word is called a pronoun. Pronouns are used to avoid repeating the same nouns in a sentence. The noun is an integral part of the sentence and can be implied from the use of the verb conjugation in the sentence. This is often the case in the 3rd person verb forms. The verb conjugation must match the number, plural or singular, of the noun which the verb modifies.

All sentences must include a noun, and when speaking Spanish, the noun is preceded by a word that identifies it as the subject called a "definite article," which can be any word meaning "the" or the "indefinite" article which can be any word meaning "a or an." The "the" words are el and la, as well as, los and las. The "a or an" words are un and una, as well as unos and unas.

For example:

La silla es blanco. The chair is white.
Unas sillas son negras. Some chairs are black.

If you are referring your own body part, use the definite article;

Me lastime la mano. I hurt my hand.

La mano is used refer a body part being spoken of on ones' own person. It is important to remember to use an article when referring to body parts.

The articles match the gender and singular or plural form of the noun being modified.

un or el for singular form, masculine
una or la for singular form, feminine
unos or los for plural form, masculine
unas or las for plural form, feminine
un or el for the neuter form (which is almost always singular)

Gender of Nouns

In Spanish, nouns have genders. The gender of the noun is important since it is the basis for the genders used by other parts of the sentence, such as the verbs and adjectives.

The gender of the noun will be either masculine, feminine, or it may be neutral. For some words, the gender will vary depending on whether you are talking about a male or a female. This is common when the noun ends in either the letter "o" when referring a male, or the letter "a" when referring a female. These nouns often relate to jobs and professions. Here are some examples:

masculine	feminine	English
el artista	la artista	the singer
el cocinero	la cocinera	the cook
el dentista	la dentista	the dentist
el estudiante	la estudiante	the student
el joven	la joven	the youth
el medico	la medica	the doctor
el modelo	la modelo	the model
el niño	la niña	the little boy/girl
el periodista	la periodista	the journalist
el telefonista	la telefonista	the operator
el dentista	la dentista	the dentist
the arquitecto	la arquitecta	the architect

There are other nouns where the article changes, but the noun itself remains the same, and the meaning of the word does not change. These nouns have an ambiguous gender like *el mar* and *la mar*. Both of these words have the same meaning, "the sea." There are other words that are treated in the same manner:

Spanish	English
el/la lente	the lens
el/la linde	the boundary
el/la maratón	the marathon
el/la vodka	the vodka
el/la web	the internet
el/la yoga	the yoga

Other words can be either feminine or masculine, but by changing the gender, the meaning of the word changes. This is true of *el cura,* which means "the priest" and *la cura,* which means 'the cure." For some words, the meaning of the word will be different if the noun is feminine than if the word is masculine. There isn't a way to determine the difference. Memorize the words and what they mean when used as either the masculine or feminine:

Spanish Word	Masculine English	Feminine English
cólera	cholera	anger
coma	coma	comma
corte	cut	court
frente	front	forehead
orden	order	decree
papa	pope	potato
parte	message	part
pendiente	earring	slope

Nouns have a gender and are either singular or plural. These must be taken into account when you construct your sentence so that you use the correct articles and pronouns to match the verb conjugations. The adjective will also match the noun it is modifying in number and gender.

In general, nouns ending in -a and -d are feminine words. All other words are usually masculine. There are some words that do not fit the general pattern, and those are noted above.

Here is the breakdown of the general rules regarding the gender of nouns:

Words ending in -n, -o, -l, -e, -r, and -s are usually masculine words. There are some exceptions, and these words will have to be memorized in order to recognize that they are exceptions.

Ending	Spanish Example	English	Exceptions	English Exceptions
-n	el ratón, el falcón	the mouse, the falcon	la imagen, la razón	the image, the rightness

-o	el gato, el libro, el aeropuerto	the cat, the book, the airport	la mano, la foto, la radio,	the hand, the photo, the radio
-l	el árbol, el papel, el sol	the tree, the paper, the sun	la cárcel, la miel, la piel	the jail, the honey, the skin
-e	el nombre	the name	la clase, la noche, la calle, la fuente	the class, the night, the street, the fountain
-r	el sabor, el corredor	the flavor, the hallway	la flor, la labor	the flower, the labor
-s	el paraguas	the umbrella	la crisis	the crisis

There are other masculine words that end in the letter "a," but are preceded by another consonant, like -ma, -pa and -ta.

Ending	Spanish Example	English	Exceptions
-ma	el drama, el clima, el poema	the drama, the climate, the poet	la pijama, la grama
-pa	el mapa	the map	la tapa, la culpa
-ta	el profeta, el planeta,	the profit, the planet	la fogata, la fiesta

Feminine words, in the singular form, end in the letters:

Ending	Spanish Example	English	Exceptions	English Exceptions
-d	la ciudad, la pared	the city, the wall	el sud, el césped	the south, the lawn
-a	la mesa, la silla, la manzana	the table, the chair, the apple	el, problema, el sofá, el tequila	the problem, the sofa, the tequila
-z	la cruz, la nuez, la voz	the cross, the nut, the voice	el lapiz, el juez, el pez	the pencil, the judge, the fish

-ie	la serie, la barbaria	the series, the barbarity		
-ión	la canción, la traducció n, la conversa ción	the song, the translati on, the conversa tion	el gorrión, el sarampi ón	the sparrow, the measles

Agreement with Verbs

Nouns are the basis of a sentence. They are the subject of the sentence and must be present, as either a noun or a pronoun, in order for the sentence to make sense. In Spanish, it is necessary for the noun, to have a numeric value of either on, which would be considered singular, or more, which is called plural. Use the verb ending that corresponds to the way the verb is used in the sentence.

Articles are also a part of the sentence, they precede the noun or pronoun. Use the corresponding article and gender of the noun or nouns. The noun may need to be modified to the correct form as well. If it needs to be changed, t should reflect the correct gender and correspond with the verb ending being used.

As an example, say, "The girls go the store," the subject is "the girls," and the verb is "go." form the sentence in Spanish, the noun will be "muchachas" which will be preceded by the article, "las." The verb will be the third person plural, "van."

Las muchachas van a la tienda.

If you say, "The man drives the car," you have to make the article singular and male by using the word "el" which has the same qualities as the verb which is in the is the one person. In Spanish, the statement is,

El hombre maneja el carro.

Notice that the verb is conjugated match the subject, and the subject matches the verb tense. In using the present and past tense of the verb forms, the noun is in front of the action word and the subject to which the action happened goes after the action word. This is demonstrated in the previous sentences. Las muchachas and El hombre are the nouns, ir and manejar are the verbs, and la tienda and el carro are the objects. The format of the sentence is Subject-Verb-Object or SVO.

It is possible to convert nouns into verbs. The conversion to the gerund tense is created by taking the root of the word and adding "ando" if the base verb is one ending in "ar." If the infinitive form of the verb ends in "er" or "ir," the gerund fund of the word adds "iendo" to the root word. "ando" and "iendo" are tantamount to the ending "ing" in English.

Example:

Let's start by selecting a noun to be converted into an action word. A *cuchara* is a spoon. We will convert it from a noun a verb, find the basis, or root, of the word which is *cuchar*. After determining the root, add the infinitive form of the word, which in this case is -ar. This forms the word, "spoon" and then makes the word, *cucharear*. The final -a in cuchara is changed an -e eliminate the -aa that would be formed. The word cuchara has been changed a verb, cucharear. By adding the gerund ending for -ar, -ando, the gerund form of the word formed is *cuchareando,* which means, spooning.

If you want to use this form of a verb, you will need to use a related form of the word "estar" as a leading verb, positioned before the gerund form of the verb:

The boy is spooning his ice cream.
El chico está cuchareando helado.

Vocabulary

Vocabulary for common nouns:

English	Spanish-Singular	Singular-Plural	Gender
air	aire	aires	m
airplane	avión	aviones	m
airport	aeropuerto	aeropuertos	m
apartment	apartamento	apartamentos	m
apple	manzana	manzanas	f
area	la zona	zonas	f
art	arte	artes	m/f
back	espalda	espaldas	f
bar	bar	barras	m
beef	carne de res	carne de res	f
beer	cerveza	cervezas	f
bicycle	bicicleta	bicicletas	f
boat	barco	barcos	m
body	cuerpo	cuerpos	m
book	libro	libros	m
box	caja	cajas	f
brandy	brandy	brandys	m

bread	un pan	panes	m
business	negocio	negocios	m
cake	pastel	pasteles	m
car	coche	coches	m
case	caso	casos	m
chair	silla	sillas	f
change	cambio	cambios	m
chicken	pollo	pollos	m
child	niño	niños	m/f
church	iglesia	iglesias	f
city	ciudad	ciudades	f
coffee	café	cafés	f
coffee shop	cafeteria	cafeterías	f
community	comunidad	comunidades	f
company	empresa	empresas	f
computer	computadora	computadores	f
country	país	países	m
countryside	campo	campos	m
croissant	cuerno	cuernos	m
day	día	días	m
desk	escritorio	escritorios	m
door	puerta	puertas	f

dress	vestir	vestidos	m
education	educación	educaciónes	f
end	final	finales	m
eye	ojo	ojos	m
face	cara	caras	f
fact	hecho	hechos	m
family	familia	familias	f
father	padre	padres	m
fish	pescado	pescados	m
force	fuerza	fuerzas	f
friend	amigo	amigos	m/f
game	juego	juegos	m
garlic	ajo	ajos	m
gin	ginebra	ginebras	f
girl	niña	niñas	f
government	gobierno	gobiernos	m
group	grupo	grupos	m
guy	chico	chicos	m
hand	mano	manos	f
head	cabeza	cabezas	f

health	salud	saludes	f
history	historia	historias	f
home	hogar	hogare	m
hotel	hotel	hoteles	m
hour	hora	horas	f
house	casa	casas	f
idea	idea	ideas	m
information	información	informaciónes	f
issue	problema	problemas	m
job	trabajo	trabajos	m
kid	niño	niños	m
kind	tipo	tipos	m
lamp	lámpara	lamparas	f
law	ley	leyes	f
lemonade	limonada	limonadas	f
level	nivel	niveles	f
life	vida	vidas	f
line	línea	líneas	f
lot	lote	lotes	m

man	hombre	hombres	m
market	mercado	mercados	f
meeting	reunión	reuniones	f
member	miembro	miembros	m
minute	minuto	minutos	m
moment	momento	momentos	m
money	dinero	dineros	m
month	mes	meses	m
morning	mañana	mañanas	f
mother	madre	madres	f
motorcycle	motocicleta	motocicletas	f
museum	museo	museos	m
name	nombre	nombres	m
night	noche	noches	f
nightclub	discoteca	discotecas	f
number	número	números	m
office	oficina	oficinas	f
olive oil	aceite de oliva	aceites de olivas	m

others	otros	otros	m/f
pants	pantalones	pantalones	m
paper	papel	documentos	m
parent	padre	padres	m
part	parte	partes	m
party	fiesta	fiestas	f
peach	durazno	duraznos	m
pen	bolígrafo	plumas	f
pencil	lápiz	lapices	f
people	personas	personas	f
person	persona	personas	f
pistachio	pistacho	pistachos	m
place	sitio	sitios	m
point	punto	puntos	m
pork	cerdo	cerdo	m
power	poder	poderes	m
presentation	presentación	presentaciones	f
president	presidente	presidentes	m
problem	problema	problemas	m
program	programa	programas	m

question	pregunta	preguntas	f
reason	razón	razones	f
research	investigación	investigaciones	f
restaurant	restaurante	restaurantes	m
result	resultado	resultados	m
right	derecha	derechas	f
road	la carretera	carreteras	f
room	habitación	habitaciones	f
salad	ensalada	ensaladas	f
sandwich	emparedado	emparedados	f
school	escuela	escuelas	f
scotch whiskey	whisky escocés	whisky escocés	m
service	servicio	servicios	m
shirt	camisa	camisas	f
shoe	zapato	zapatos	m
shorts	pantalones cortos	pantalones cortos	m
side	lado	lados	m
skirt	falda	faldas	f

sofa	sofá	sofás	m
state	estado	estados	m
store	tienda	tiendas	f
story	cuenta	cuentas	f
student	estudiante	estudiantes	m/f
suit	traje	trajes	m
system	sistema	sistemas	f
table	mesa	mesas	f
taxi	taxi	taxis	m
tea	té	tés	m
teacher	profesor	profesores	m/f
team	equipo	equipos	m
thing	cosa	cosas	f
toilet	baño	baños	m
tomato	tomate	tomates	m
train	tren	trenes	m
truck	camión	camiones	f
t-shirt	camiseta	camisetas	f
village	pueblo	pueblos	m
vineyard	viñedo	viñedos	m
vodka	vodka	vodkas	f
war	guerra	guerras	f
water	agua	aguas	f

way	camino	caminos	m
week	semana	semanas	f
wine	vino	vinos	m
woman	mujer	mujeres	f
word	palabra	palabras	f
work	trabajo	trabajos	m
world	mundo	mundos	m
year	año	años	m

Food	Singular	Plural	Gen der
the almond	la almendra	las almendras	f
the apple	la manzana	las manzanas	f
the beef	la carne	las carne	f
the bread	el pan	los panes	m
the cake	el pastel	los pasteles	m
the candy	el caramelo	Los dulces	m
the chicken	el pollo	los pollos	m
the chocolate	el chocolate	los chocolates	m
the garlic	el ajo	los ajos	m

the lemon	el limón	las limonadas	m
the lime	la lima	las limas	f
the peach	el durazno	los duraznos	m
the pork	el puerco	los porks	m
the salad	la ensalada	las ensaladas	f
the tomato	el tomate	los tomates	m
Drinks	**Singular**	**Plural**	**Gen der**
the beer	la cerveza	las cervezas	f
the coffee	el café	los cafés	m
the juice	el jugo	los jugos	m
the milk	la leche	las leches	f
the rum	el ron	los rones	m
the soda	el refresco	los refrescos	m
the tequila	el tequila	los tequilas	m
the tonic water	el agua tónica	las aguas tónicas	m
the wine	el vino	los vinos	m
Clothes	**Singular**	**Plural**	**Gen**

			der
the boot	la bota	las botas	f
the coat	el abrigo	los abrigos	m
the dress	el vestido	los vestidos	m
the jacket	la chaqueta	las chaquetas	f
the scarf	la bufanda	las bufandas	f
the sock	el calcetín	los calcetines	m
the sweater	el suéter	los suéteres	m
the tie	la corbata	las corbatas	f
Settings	**Singular**	**Plural**	**Gen der**
the city	la ciudad	las ciudades	f
the countryside	el campo	los campos	m
the road	el camino	los caminos	m
the village	la aldea	los pueblos	f
the vineyard	el viñedo	los viñedos	m
Buildings	**Singular**	**Plural**	**Gen der**

the apartment	el apartamento	los apartamentos	m
the bar	el bar	los bares	m
the cemetary	el cementerio	los cementerios	m
the church	la iglesia	las iglesias	f
the garage	el garaje	los garajes	m
the gas station	la gasolinera	las estaciones de servicio	f
the hair salon	la peluquería	las peluquerías	f
the hospital	el hospital	los hospitales	m
the hotel	el hotel	los hoteles	m
the market	el mercado	los mercados	m
the movie theater	el cine	los cines	m
the office	la oficina	las oficinas	f
the restaurant	el restaurante	los restaurantes	m
the university	la universidad	las universidades	f

Furniture	Singular	Plurals	Gender
the bed	la cama	las camas	f
the chair	la silla	las sillas	f
the desk	el escritorio	los escritorios	m
the lamp	la lámpara	las lamparas	f
the piano	el piano	los pianos	m
the television	la televisión	la televisiónes	f

Office	Singular	Plural	Gender
the computer	la computadora	las computadoras	f
the copier	la copiadora	las copiadoras	f
the meeting	la reunión	las reuniones	f
the printer	la impresora	las impresoras	f
the report	el informe	los informes	m
the stapler	la engrapadora	las grapadoras	f

Transportation	Singular	Plural	Gender
the airplane	el avión	los aviones	m
the bicycle	la bicicleta	las bicicletas	f
the boat	el barco	los botes	m
the helicopter	el helicóptero	los helicópteros	m
the rollerskates	el patino	los patines	m
the moped	el ciclomotor	los ciclomotores	m
the train	el tren	los trenes	m
the truck	el camión	los camiones	m

This covers a lot of nouns that can be used in speaking Spanish. These words can be easily combined with the basic verbs to form simple sentences. Remember the basic word order of a Spanish sentence. The subject goes first, then the verb, then the object. When there is a pronoun in the sentence, it goes in front of the verb. Let's compare a simple sentence in English to a simple sentence in Spanish; pay attention to the differences in structure and word order.

English   **Spanish**

| They eat apples. | *Ellos comen las manzanas.* |
| He eats pork. | *Él come carne puerco.* |

When there is a pronoun like "ellos" and "él," the pronoun is placed in the sentence prior to a verb and serves as the theme of the sentence. Without the proper placement, the sentence may be written with incorrect syntax and the meaning portrayed may be different than intended.

It is also important to remember to use the accents properly to avoid confusion in pronouncing some words and defining other words. In the sentences above, the word "él" has an accent over the letter "e" for the word mean "he." Without the accent, the word "el" means "the."

Chapter 4: Adjectives Provide the Details

An adjective is a modifier that works as a descriptor in a sentence. Use the adjective to modify the subject. By modify, I mean clarifies. The adjective describes the subject of the sentence and may serve to clarify the subject as well. Adjectives are used to describe how the subject appears, feels or seems. They provide the details that make your sentences interesting and will be used on a regular basis.

Placement in Sentences

Adjectives are placed after the word they are modifying in Spanish. For example, if you are using the adjective "red" to describe a dress you want to purchase, you would use the S.V.O. method to form the sentence, and then add the adjective after the word being described:

English	Spanish
I want to buy the red dress.	*Quiero comprar el vestido rojo.*
The white dog is running.	*Corre la perra blanca.*

The adjectives above are red and white. These words are placed after the items being described—in this case, the dress and the dog. There may be more than one adjective in a sentence. It is important to follow the subject being modified by the adjective immediately so you can easily identify the correct subject.

English
Spanish
The blue sky has fluffy clouds.   *El cielo azul tiene nubes esponjosas.*
The small monkey has yellow teeth.   *El mono pequeño tiene dientes amarillos.*

The sky is blue, *azul,* and the clouds are fluffy, *esponjosas.* The monkey is small, or *pequeño,* and its teeth are yellow, or *amarillos.* In the sentences, the adjectives are right after the subject, so the description is easily applied to the correct word in the sentence.

Agreement with Nouns and Verbs

Just like nouns, adjectives must agree with the gender and number of the subjects and verbs in the sentence. So, if the subject being modified is a singular, masculine subject, the adjective will be as well.

For example, the noun *las paredes, "the walls,"* is feminine and plural. As a result, the adjective must be feminine and plural and placed after the subject. Using this in a sentence:

English
Spanish
The striped walls are pretty.   *Las paredes rayadas están bonitas.*
The red leaves fall off the tree.   *Las ojas rojas se caen del arbol.*

The adjectives used above, *rayadas, bonitas,* and *rojas* are all derived from words ending in -o. The base words are *rayado, bonito,* and *rojo.* The forms of these endings are changed to match the subject as well as the verb form. Below is a guideline for the endings of adjectives.

Adjectives ending in:

Ending	Sing. Masc.	Plu. Masc.	Sing. Fem.	Plu. Fem.
-o	-o *perro blanco* white dog	-os *perro blancos* white dogs	-a *lapiz* *amaril la* yellow pencil	-as *lapices* *amarill as* yellow pencils
-e	-e *hombre interesa nte* interesti ng man	-es *hombres interesan tes* interestin g men	-e *mujer triste* sad woman	-es *mujeres tristes* sad women
-ista	-ista *padre extremis ta* extreme father	-istas *padres extremist as* extreme fathers	-ista *madre s* *idealis ta* idealist ic mother	-istas *madres idealist as* idealisti c mother s
consona nt	(no ending) *gajoven* young	-es *gatos jovenes* young	(no ending) *casa azul* blue	-es *casas azules* blue

	cat	cats	house	house

In changing a word from singular to plural, special treatment for some words is exactly the same. For words ending in **zeta**, the **zeta** is changed to **ce** and followed by the plural ending of "*es.*"

Sometimes, it is preferable to state the state or condition of the subject by using a verb form of "be." In Spanish, that would be the words *estar* and *ser*. The general rule when deciding whether to use *estar* or *ser* is that *estar* is used for temporary conditions and *ser* is used for permanent conditions.

Below is a list of words that only use "ser," only use "estar," and some using both.

Ser	Estar	Ser y Estar
Común	Acostumbrado	Abierto
Conocido	Bien	Bueno
Contrario	Contento	Cerrado
Importante	Convencido	Listo
Posible	Escondido	Malo
Suficiente	Preocupado	Moreno
Único	Prohibido	Rico

Vocabulary

Spanish	English

abierto	open
actual	current
alto	high
amarillo	yellow
americano	american
azul	blue
bajo	low
blanco	white
bonito	nice
bueno	good
caliente	hot
central	central
cerca	close
cierto	true
cierto	certain
claro	clear
contento	happy
corto	short
derecha	right
diferente	different
difícil	hard
especial	special
fácil	easy
final	final

físico	physical
frío	cold
fuerte	strong
general	general
grande	big
grande	large
gratis	free
grave	serious
humano	human
importante	important
incorrecto	wrong
internacional	international
izquierda	left
joven	young
largo	long
legal	legal
listo	ready
lleno	full
local	local
malo	bad
mayor	major
médico	medical
mejor	best
mejor	better

militar	military
muerto	dead
multa	fine
nacional	national
natural	natural
negro	black
nuevo	new
oscuro	dark
otro	other
pasado	past
pequeño	small
pequeño	little
personal	personal
pobre	poor
poder	able
popular	popular
posible	possible
principal	main
privado	private
probable	likely
público	public
real	real
reciente	recent
religioso	religious

rojo	red
seguro	sure
sencillo	simple
significativo	significant
similar	similar
social	social
solamente	only
soltero	single
tarde	late
temprano	early
todo	all
tradicional	traditional
varios	various
verde	green
viejo	old

Chapter 5: Common Phrases, Idioms, and Dialogue

In any language, there are basic common phrases that need to be used to communicate. Let's start with questions and phrases that are commonly used in the Spanish language.

Common Phrases and Questions

Below are common phrases you will find useful in speaking Spanish:

English	Spanish
Hello	Hola
How are you?	¿Cómo estás?
I am fine.	Estoy bien.
Where are you going?	¿A dónde vas?
Do you understand?	Lo entiendes?
I don't understand.	No entiendo.
Where is the bus?	¿Donde esta el bus?
Where is the train?	¿Dónde está el tren?
How do you get to the airport?	¿Cómo se llega al aeropuerto?
How is the weather?	¿Como está el clima?

It is raining.	Llueve.
It is snowing.	Está nevando.
It is sunny.	Hace sol.
Do you want to go to the movies?	¿Quieres ir al cine?
Do you want to go dancing?	¿Quieres ir a bailar?
Call me when you arrive.	Llámame cuando llegues.
What time is it?	¿Que hora es?
It is three o'clock.	Son las tres en punto.
It is 2:30.	Son las 2:30.
Where it the beach?	Donde esta la playa?
Do you know how ski?	¿Sabes esquiar?
How old are you?	¿Cuantos años tienes?
Where is the church?	¿Dónde está la Iglesia?
Where is the museum?	¿Donde esta el museo?
Is it too far walk?	¿Es demasiado lejos para ir caminando?
Can I see your identification?	¿Puedo ver tu identificación?

Do you have a room availaible?	¿Tiene una habitación disponible?
Is there a taxi?	¿Hay un taxi?
Happy birthday!	¡feliz cumpleaños!
Please direct me to the bathroom.	Por favor, llévame al baño.

Common Greetings

Buenas Dias! Como se llama? Como esta?

A greeting is the best way to start any conversation. You may not know what say afterword, but it's good manners say hello.

English	Spanish
Hello	Hola
Good morning	Buenas dias
Good night	Buenas noches
Goodbye	Adios
Good Luck	Buena suerte

As you can see, the word "bueno" is an adjective that is modified to match the subject. By pairing it with the correct subject, you have the correct greeting the situation requires. Practice the greetings in a sentence, and think of normal situations where you would use a greeting. Here is a conversation that you may have had in English several times:

Hola, Ricardo. Tienes tiempo ir para tomar cafe?
>-*Hi, friend. Do you have time for coffee?*

Buenas dias, amiga. Vamos a Starbucks.
>-*Good morning, friend. Let's go to Starbucks.*

Even if you are not conversing with friends, by using a greeting, you will be more likely to get a response. This will be especially useful while traveling if you are not confident with your Spanish skills. It is a way to ease into interacting with people. Your vocabulary will increase as you speak with more people, so it is advantageous to start chatting with a simple, "Hello." If you are lucky enough to be on your journey to master Spanish with others, there is ample opportunity to practice using the language in common conversations. Just use the words you know and practice using them in any way you can.

The conversation above is geared towards people you already know. Now, let's look at how to have conversations with people you haven't met or are meeting for the first time. You may need to learn their names. Let's go over how to ask people their names and how you tell people your name.

The phrase for asking a person's name is actually "How are you called?" The chart below will give you an idea of how to meet people and introduce yourself. Remember, in Spanish, there are informal and formal ways to address people. show respect, use the formal, or 3rd person, form of the verb *llamarse*. If you are speaking with someone of a similar age or status, it is okay to use the 2nd person forms of the verbs. Use your judgment and remember to use good manners. Every community may not be as informal as you are used to.

English	Spanish
What's your name? (informal)	¿Como te llamas?
(formal)	¿Como se llama??
(multiple people)	¿Como se llaman?
What is his name?	¿Como se llama él?
My name is Laura.	Me llamo Laura.
My name is Mrs. Jones. Jones.	Me llamo Sra.
We are the Hamiltons.	Nos llamamos la familia Hamilton.
His name is George.	Èl se llama George.

It is a good idea to practice these questions and answers with different people and get into the habit of using different tenses and verb forms. It is especially easy to forget to use formal tenses in today's informal society. You will always be able to modify each individual situation, depending on the people involved. Be comfortable with all the forms, so the phrases roll from your mind easily and do not require a lot of thought. Because it is such a basic situation, you will have plenty of opportunities to meet people and introduce yourself. The formal tense is used in work situations as well as when meeting older people. If you are asked your name, it is appropriate to respond with the same degree of respect if returning the same question.Be prepared by knowing the various verb tenses.

After meeting people, it will be normal to exchange pleasantries regarding the well-being of the people you have just met. They will also ask about you.

English	Spanish
How are you? (informal)	¿Cómo estas?
	¿Cómo está usted? (formal)
How are we?	¿Cómo estamos?
How are you all? ustedes?	¿Cómo están

The question is simple and common. The verb tense of *estar,* be, is used to show who is being asked the question. Here are some common answers to the question:

I'm doing well!	¡Estoy bien!
It's fine!	¡Esta bien!
I feel bad!	¡Estoy mala!
Okay.	Asì asì.
Pretty good, thanks!	Estoy bien, gracias.
Great!	¡Muy bien!

You can always elect to say "thank you." You are already familiar with the word, *gracias*. People appreciate a thank you almost all the time. Sometimes you will be gender-specific in using the adjective, and your adjective will also be singular or plural. Follow the rules outlined under the section on adjectives use the proper form of the adjective in your description. If you want to use an exclamation point, remember to put an exclamation point at the beginning of the phrase as well as the end when writing the response in Spanish.

Numeros (Numbers)

Below is a chart that illustrates numbers and outlines the pronunciation of them. Of course, numbers are used every day, so it will be important to learn the numbers, but easy at the same time. By memorizing the numbers one through ten, you will be well on your way knowing the numbers and how to pronounce them as well. You can practice them in your mind on a daily basis; for example, when thinking of the number in English, translate it to Spanish so that in the future, the Spanish version of English numbers comes to you easily. After the number 20, when you want to say 21, simply think in your mind that the number is 20 and 1, or *veinte y uno*. Replace the letter y with the letter i and make it one word, *veintiuno*. This is followed by *veintidos*, *veintitres*, etc.

0	cero	say-row
1	uno	oo-nowh
2	dos	dohws
3	tres	trays
4	cuatro	kwat-roh
5	cinco	sink-oh
6	seis	sehs
7	siete	cee-ehh-tay
8	ocho	o-chohh
9	nueve	nu-a-bay
10	diez	d-ase
11	once	owhn-sahy
12	doce	dos-ay
13	trece	trays-ahy
14	catorce	kahh-TORH-sahy

15	quince	KEYN-sahy
16	dieciséis	d-EHZ-hee-sehs
17	diecisiete	d-EHZ-hee-cee ehh-tahy
18	dieciocho	d-EHZ-cee-o-chohh
19	diecinueve	d-EHZ-cee-nu-a-bay
20	veinte	VANE-tahy
30	treinta	trayn-tdah
40	cuarenta	kwar-EHN- tdah
50	cincuenta	sen-KWEN- tdah
60	sesenta	sahy-SIHN- tdah
70	setenta	sahy-TIHN- tdah
80	ochenta	o-CHEN- tdah
90	noventa	nhoh-VIHN-tah
100	cien	scee-IN
200	docientos	doh-seeh-IN-tdohs
300	tresientos	tray-seeh-IN- tdohs
400	cuatrocientos	kwah-tro-seeh-IN-tdohs
500	quinientos	Keeh-knee-IN- tdohs
600	seiscientos	says-seeh-IN- tdohs

700	setecientos	seht-a-see-IN- tdohs
800	ochocientos	o-choh-seeh-IN- tdohs
900	novecientos	noh-bay-seeh-IN-tdohs
1000	mil	meehl
2000	dos mil	dohs-meehl
3000	tres mil	trays-meehl

¿Qué te gusta? (What Do You Like?)

The verb gustarse is used to ask what a person likes. Put the object in front of the verb. In answer, place the object in front of the correct tense of *gustar*. That way, you are saying, "me, I like..." instead of the English way which says "I like...." You must use the plural or singular version of *gustar* to match the numeric value in conjugating *gustar*. For the singular, if you like one thing, it is *gusta*. For the plural, if you like more than one thing, it is *gustan*.

English
I like my dog.
I like dogs.

Spanish
Me gusta mi perro.
Me gustan los perros.

When you ask people what they like, they tend to answer. It is a way to engage people while also expanding your knowledge of the Spanish language. Let's look at some of the things people like do:

English	Spanish
sports	deportes
game	juego
football (soccer)	fútbol
football (American)	fútbol americano
baseball	béisbol
tennis	tenis
chess	ajedrez
backgammon	chaquete
winners	ganadores
losers	perdedores

There are many things people like do, they like play (jugar), watch TV (guardar la television), read (leer), and sing (cantar).

English	Spanish
Do you like to sing?	¿Te gusta cantar?
Yes, I like to sing.	Sí, me gusta cantar.
Do you like sandia?	¿Te gusta la sandia?
Yes, I like watermelon. sandia.	Sí, mi piace la
Do you like my earrings? pendientes?	¿Te gustan mis
I don't like your earrings. gustan tus pendientes.	No, a mi no me

This is a nice conversation starter. You are asking about another person, and most people like to talk about themselves. You can use your list of vocabulary words to substitute the object when asking what people like. You have also been supplied with the format for responding. So you not only know what to say but how to say it. The formats for answering yes and no have been provided. There is also the format for singular and plural. Simply use different vocabulary words to find out what interests people have and what they like. Be ready to respond with something you like. It is a great way to be involved in a conversation in a different language. They will be simple sentences, but effective in conveying information.

Back the Basics

After all the talk of grammar and sentence structure, there are some words that are commonly used that we have yet cover. Let's go over some of them so that they are fresh in your mind.

English	Spanish
Monday	lunes
Tuesday	martes
Wednesday	miércoles
Thursday	jueves
Friday	viernes
Saturday	sábado
Sunday	domingo

What do you notice about the days of the week written in Spanish? That's right; there are no capital letters used. The only reason to use a capital letter referring to a day is if it is the first word of a sentence. To pronounce the days, the same rules as normal apply, and the penultimate syllable is stressed unless there is an accent indicate the stress is on a different syllable.

Also related the days of the week, here are a few more words:

English	Spanish
tomorrow	mañana
today	hoy
yesterday	ayer

The months of the year are as follows:

English	Spanish
January	enero
February	febrero
March	marzo
April	abril
May	mayo
June	junio
July	julio
August	agosto
September	septiembre
October	octubre
November	noviembre
December	diciembre

The same rules of capitalization apply as with the days. They are not normally capitalized in the Spanish language. Many of the months have similar sounds and are easily recognizable in writing. The natural accent will prevail and be placed on the penultimate syllable to correctly pronounce thee months. If you want to write the date, for the long form of the date, place, and article, the numeric day followed by the word "*de*," the month "*de*," and the year. So, say Christmas 2019, the date is "*el 25 de enero 2019.*"

Here are a few sentences, questions, and responses involving days, months and years:

English Spanish
Let's go to the movies Monday night. Vamos al cine en Lunes.
-I'm busy Monday. Let's go Tuesday. – *Estoy ocupado. Vamos en martes.*
When is your birthday? ¿Cuando es tu cumpleaños?
-My birthday is April 15. -Mi cumpleaños es el 15 de abril.
What is today's date? ¿Cual es la fecha hoy?
-Today is January 15, 2020 -Hoy es el 15 de enero de 2020.

Knowing the days of the week and the months of the year will come in handy whether you are traveling, chatting with a native or practicing with your friends and colleagues. Just remember that the days of the weeks and months are not capitalized when writing in Italian unless they are the first word of a sentence.

Las Estaciones del Año (Seasons of the Year)

The seasons are not capitalized either. It seems as though many of these items are more descriptive rather than the official name of a season. So the capitalization is forgone.

English	Spanish
Summer	verano
Autumn	atoño
Winter	inverno
Spring	primavera

The Spanish language is native to several different countries on different continents. As a result, there are variances in the seasons that coincide with the particular hemisphere and locations. In Spain, the summer months are usually considered to be June, July, and August. Autumn is September, October, and November. Winter starts in December, lasting through March, and the spring is April, May, and June. This is true of Spanish speaking countries in North and Central America as well. In South America, the seasons are reversed. When it is summer in North America, it is Winter in the southern tip of Argentina. There are vast differences in the weather and climate for all the different countries where Spanish is the native language. In Mexico and Spain, there is often a traditional mid-day break between 1 pm and 3 pm. For these two hours, some people retire their homes to eat a meal and stay cool. This is generally considered a traditional siesta but isn't as necessary now with the changes lifestyles and accessibility of air conditioning.

El Cuerpo (The Body)

Parts of the body are spoken of in the third person. When you are talking about a specific part of the body, the grammar is that of an indirect object. Precede the vocabulary body part with an article. The sentence is correct if you say "the finger" and not "my finger."

My arm hurts.
   -*Me duele el brazo.*

English	Spanish
leg	pierna
foot	pie
hair	pelo
chest	pecho
belly	panza
ear	oreja
eye	ojo
nose	nariz
hand	mano
back	espalda
finger	dedo

face	cara
head	cabeza
arm	brazo
mouth	boca
chin	barbilla

Mira Los Colores del Arco Iris (Look at the Colors of the Rainbow)

Colors are adjectives. Follow the same rules as you do with all other adjectives. The number and gender of the verb and subject must be reflected in the Since colors are adjectives, you must match the ending of the adjective the noun and verbs being modified. Follow the rules outlined in the sections above to determine how to pluralize and assign gender the colors. Review the following sentences as examples of how the colors match the nouns and verbs in the sentences.

The brown cow has big eyes.
   -*La vaca marrón tiene ojos grandes.*

The white bull does not like me.
   - *El toro blanco no me gusta.*

I see two red balloons.
   -*Veo unos dos globos rojos.*

Because the word for "brown" ends in the letter "n" it does not change with the feminine subject. You can see from the examples that the ending for the color brown does not change for gender, but it would change for a plural subject by adding -es. The cow is brown (*marrón*, singular female) and the bull is white (blanco, singular male). The adjective ending in "e" and "a" are gender-neutral (like grande) and they do not change for gender. The numeric value matches the subject, "ojos."

The basic color vocabulary list is below. Just remember, colors are simply adjective and follow the rules of all other adjectives:

English	Spanish
black	negro
blue	azul
brown	marrón
green	verde
grey	gris
orange	naranja
pink	rosado
purple	púrpura
red	rojo
white	blanco
yellow	amarillo

Preguntas (Questions)

We have already asked many questions, but here is a summary of the question words that are commonly used in the Spanish language.

When you are learning a new language, there will be lots of questions. If you are traveling, questions are often the only way to get the information needed. A good way to practice speaking the language you are learning is to ask and answer questions. It is a built-in guide to conversations. If you are asked a question, you will want to know how to answer. People will feel compelled to respond if you ask questions of them. There have already been a lot of questions in this book; now, let's get a list of interrogative words all in one place for easy reference.

English	Spanish
What?	¿Qué?
Why?	¿Por qué?
When?	¿Cuando?
Where?	¿Dónde?
How?	¿Cómo?
How much?	¿Cuáncuesta?
How many?	¿Cuántos?
Who?	Quien?

When asking a question about someone or something, a personal pronoun may be necessary. If this is the case, the personal pronoun goes at the end of the phrase. It is the same as the English language, so it's easy to see when the two sentences are side-by-side:

English	Spanish
Where is she?	¿Donde esta ella?
Who lives there?	¿Quien vive allí?
How is he?	¿Como es el?

In the questions above, the word that asks the questions lead the phrase. They start off, the verb follows the interrogative word and the personal pronoun is at the end of the question. This should be comfortable for you since it is exactly the same as the English language questions.

A key difference between asking a question in English versus the Spanish language question is the preposition. It is not uncommon to end a question with a preposition when asking a question in English. In Spanish, this is not the case. For instance, in speaking English, it is not uncommon to say, "Who will I go the movies with?" This is not the case in Spanish since the preposition will go in front of the interrogative, "¿Con quien voy al cine?" The Spanish preposition goes the head of the sentence.

Conclusion

The next step is to continue practicing the dialogue and conversation in this book. By repeating the phrases and sentences outlined above, you will become more comfortable speaking Spanish and have a better understanding of the language when you hear it. Practice making your own sentences using the information on sentence structure and the vocabulary. Work on simple sentences. All you need is a noun and a verb to create a sentence. You can start speaking Spanish right away.

Thank You

I would like to thank you from the bottom of my heart for coming along with me on this investing journey. There are many books out there, but you decided to give this one a chance.

If you liked this book, then I need your help!

Please take a moment to leave an honest review of this book. This feedback gives me a good understanding of the kinds of books and topics readers want to read about and it will also give my book more visibility.

Leaving a review takes less than one minute and is much appreciated.